SAN JOSE

City With A Past

SAN JOSE

City With A Past

Kathleen Muller

Foreword by Mayor Tom McEnery

*This limited edition was printed in 1988 as a
membership premium by The San Jose Historical Museum Association
635 Phelan Avenue • San Jose, CA 95112*

Printed in USA by
The Rosicrucian Press
76 Notre Dame Avenue

Editor: Kathleen Muller

Limited first edition, 1988
Published by the San Jose Historical Museum Association

Foreword

There is an old photograph of Downtown San Jose that is quite familiar to those with even a cursory knowledge of local history. I was glancing at a book the other day and once again it jumped out at me, but this time in quite a different way. The photo presents a wonderful scene of merriment and ceremony: police officers on horseback, trolley cars jammed with riders, children holding balloons, families at ease, people enjoying their City. A few weeks ago, I saw virtually the same scene in our present City: cops and balloons, ice cream cones and children, parasols and trolleys. Even some of the buildings and street signs were the same. It brought home something that we all know instinctively, namely, that the place we live in and enjoy today is not only built on the past, but that in the truest sense, "it is the past". When we proudly sit in the lobby of the Fairmont Hotel, we sit a few feet above a kaleidoscope of San Jose history. Located here was the San Jose Creamery of my grandfather "Honest Ben" Sellers, and the old Padre Theatre where many wiled away a Saturday afternoon. It was also the site of the vacant lots and vanquished hopes of many failed Redevelopment policies in our "locust years". Here, too, was the location of the unofficial City Hall of "Boss" Charley Bigley's ambulance company. One hundred years ago, one of the largest Chinese settlements in California thrived on this very spot, and thirty-five years before that, the roof of the State Capitol covered a building better known as the "Legislature of a Thousand Drinks". Conquistadors and pioneers, prune growers and politicians, and those just seeking an ice cream soda, have called this one block of our City their own, for the hour, for the moment, or to the bottom of a soda glass.

Things, of course, change. Nowhere is that more reliable and relevant than in this special Valley. Although much has been altered in San Jose, it is very easy to see the City of another time wherever you walk in the Downtown: in street names, in the blossoms of a tree, or in a building facade.

It is going to be very interesting to look at the following pictures of the old Downtown, interspersed with the new. Perhaps the greatest fun, and certainly the most evocative, will be the association of people, friends and trailblazers, with the memories, street scenes and structures on these pages. Captain Thomas Fallon's estate, J. J. Owen's revolutionary Light Tower, Bob Benson's Studebaker dealerships, the old St. Joseph's of Fathers Ring and McQuillan, Jay McCabe's Civic Auditorium complex, Vic Corsiglia's San Antonio Street office, the First National Bank corner office of the Oneal clan, Don Goldeen's furniture store on South First Street, the Farmers Union and the Sainte Claire Hotel, Hart's and W. H. Weeks' De Anza Hotel—each have their own stories and their own unique set of memories.

We will see very clearly that we all live in the center of our own book, with many chapters preceding us and many just as surely to follow. As we look at the images of the past, juxtaposed with current sights, we know with certainty that we are today living and building our own history.

Tom Mc Sy

Thomas P. McEnery
Mayor of San Jose

Introduction

San Jose: **City With A Past** is an effort to examine the changing faces of Downtown San Jose. The impetus behind this examination is the emergence of a "new" Downtown during the 1980s and our belief that knowledge of the City's rich past will help us more fully appreciate the present.

This is, of course, an overview, limited by the historic images that were available. We concentrated on selecting photographs of significant buildings, street scenes that reflected the size and nature of the City, and particular locations that have been central to the City's life over the years. We strove to illustrate the growth and development of San Jose in the early years, the bustling heyday of the Downtown, its subsequent decline and recent rebirth.

For the purpose of this project, Downtown is the area bounded by the Guadalupe River on the west, 10th Street on the east, Julian Street on the north and Reed Street on the south.

Virtually all of the historic photographs were drawn from the Archives of the San Jose Historical Museum. For many of the modern photographs we are deeply indebted to Barbara J. Dorr, retired photographer for the County of Santa Clara, who donated her time and talent to photograph particular scenes. We also wish to acknowledge the cooperation and contributions of Del Carlo Photography, Rick Donner of Bank of the West, Sharon Hall Photography, Leonard McKay, the San Jose Mercury News, and the City of San Jose Redevelopment Agency.

Photographs of San Jose today were also gathered through a contest sponsored by the San Jose Historical Museum Association to involve the community in the revival of Downtown and to see the City through the eyes of its citizens. The most representative of the photographs are included in this publication, but all of the entries have become a part of the Museum's Archives, to provide a record of San Jose today for future scholars and historians.

Frank Taylor, Director of the San Jose Redevelopment Agency; Ron James, President of the Chamber of Commerce; Albert Dixon, Director of the San Jose Museum of Art; and Al Magazu, from Superior Color Lab in San Jose are gratefully acknowledged as honorary judges of the contemporary photo contest.

Mignon Gibson, Director of the San Jose Historical Museum, and the members of the Museum Association's Publication Committee were a tremendous support in this project. My special thanks go to Patricia Loomis, writer of many years for the *San Jose Mercury News*. Her knowledge of local history, love of San Jose, and eagerness to contribute to this project were qualities I leaned on heavily. In addition, Leslie Masunaga, Archivist, and Nancy Valby, Curator, from the staff of the San Jose Historical Museum, were instrumental in the production of this publication from start to finish and I am grateful for their enormous contributions.

Finally, we all hope that this cursory look at the history of the Downtown will leave you with an understanding that life has existed in the area we call Downtown San Jose, constantly changing, since before the coming of the Spanish in the 18th Century. We are merely the latest chapter in a long, continuing line of people who have lived and worked here, making San Jose our home. What we are creating today will tell future generations much about our lifestyle and values as a community.

Kathleen Muller

Contents

1st St
San Jose

Spanish Pueblo to American City
1777 - 1885

Named after St. Joseph, patron saint of the Spanish expedition to California, the Pueblo de San Jose de Guadalupe, the first civil settlement in California, was founded on November 29, 1777. Lieutenant Don Jose Joaquin Moraga of the Presidio of San Francisco established the little settlement of 66 persons on the east bank of the Guadalupe River (between the river, Hedding Street, Hobson Street and First Street).

In 1797 the settlement was moved about one mile south, since dams built on the Guadalupe River failed to control flooding. Pueblo life centered around the plaza which was surrounded by lots for the council house, church, storerooms, and other public buildings. Boundaries of the new town extended from just north of St. John Street to just south of San Carlos Street and from San Pedro Street to the east line of Market Street.

The Spanish objective in establishing the pueblo at San Jose was to support the presidios at Monterey and San Francisco. Through food production, the supply of horses to the cavalry, and the creation of a civilian population, the pueblo complemented the other Spanish efforts at colonization.

In 1846 Thomas Fallon raised the American flag over San Jose, establishing American control over the pueblo which since 1822 had been governed by Mexico.

Looking north on First Street from Santa Clara Street in the 1870s. The Bank of San Jose building, built in 1872, stands prominently on the northeast corner. Building to the right, housing George H. Hare Books & Stationery on the ground floor, is the Commercial and Savings Bank. Feist Brothers Dry Goods is on the northwest corner of the intersection.

When the first Constitutional Convention met in Monterey and designated San Jose the state capital of California, the population of the city numbered almost 3,000. By the time the first Legislature convened in San Jose on December 15, 1849, the population had jumped to 4,000.

The Legislature met in a hastily constructed two-story adobe structure located on the east side of the plaza. The citizens of San Jose were hospitable, but the winter of 1849-50 proved to be an extremely rainy one. The legislators, tired of mud, flooded streets and inadequate accommodations, voted to move the state capital to Vallejo in 1851.

Early photographs show that by 1850 wooden buildings were being constructed adjacent to the adobes of the old pueblo. The City of San Jose was incorporated on March 27, 1850 (and reincorporated March 27, 1857) and the first City Hall was built at 35 North Market Street in 1855. The only structures remaining in Downtown San Jose from this very early period are the Peralta Adobe and the home of Thomas Fallon, located directly across from each other on St. John Street.

During the decade of the 1860s San Jose was improving its streets, building its first streetcar line, new hotels, and a Courthouse building that was designed to lure the state capital back to San Jose. Commercial movement onto First Street was beginning.

Wheat was the main product of the area's agricultural economy and San Jose was the market place for the entire county. The city boasted a half dozen flour mills in the 1850s and '60s. The railroad was completed from San Francisco to San Jose in 1864 and the opening of the transcontinental railroad in 1868 enabled growers in San Jose to ship their products on a larger scale. Orchards began replacing grain fields in the 1870s and by 1876 San Jose was the fruit shipping capital of California.

During the 1870s, San Jose's population rapidly increased. The State Normal School was located here, canneries were started, and businesses began to overflow from First Street onto Second Street. A steam-powered street car line was built along First Street in the early part of the decade and the first telephone exchange came in (with five subscribers) on March 10, 1879.

A 237-foot Electric Light Tower was constructed in 1881, straddling the intersection of Market and Santa Clara Streets, and providing the City of San Jose with a landmark for which it became known worldwide. The inspiration of San Jose Mercury newspaper owner J. J. Owen, the tower served as the central feature of Downtown and as the symbol of San Jose for over thirty years. It was the most powerful concentration of electric light in America at the time.

NORTH 5TH ST.

NORTH 4TH ST.

NORTH 3RD ST.

PRESENT LOCATION
ST. CLAIRE CLUB

N. 2ND ST.

E. ST. JAMES ST.

ST. JAMES PARK

241

SAN JOSE IN THE "FIFTIES"

An early photograph of San Jose in the 1850s shows the layout of streets prior to the development of St. James Park. Notations in white ink were made on the original photograph.

The La Serena Adobe, located at Market and San Carlos Streets, was typical of adobe structures from the Pueblo era. Erected by John Deaver at a cost of $1200, this adobe rented for $80 a month in 1852, according to a note on the back of the original photograph.

13

An early photograph of Market Street and the Plaza, probably dating from the mid-1860s. To the left of the curve is the present site of the Fairmont Hotel. Note the City's commercial water tanks.

14

Looking east toward the Santa Clara Street School which stands prominently in the background of this photograph. The school was built in 1866 at Santa Clara and 15th Streets. In March 1892 the Santa Clara Street School was renamed Horace Mann School.

San Jose in the late 1860s. Looking east, the church in the background is the First Presbyterian Church located on Second Street and erected in 1863.

This classic Corinthian County Courthouse building, designed by Levi Goodrich and first occupied in 1868, still stands on North First Street across from St. James Park. The original dome, shown in this early photograph, collapsed in a 1931 fire and was not replaced when the building was remodeled at that time. Note the young trees of St. James Park.

Looking west on Santa Clara Street from the corner of First, about 1870. Feist's Dry Goods (pictured at the right) was on the corner of First and Santa Clara. The Auzerais House, built for $150,000 by Theodore Lenzen, was San Jose's largest building and the county's finest hotel when it opened on March 16, 1865.

The 1855 City Hall, at what later became 35 North Market Street. It was a two-story brick structure with council chambers on the ground floor and two small rooms and an assembly hall upstairs. The county leased the second floor as a courtroom for a short time but the lease was not renewed in 1862 because the city needed the space.

The recently incorporated Farmer's Union occupied this building at Second and Santa Clara Streets in 1874. The building had recently been purchased from Adolph Pfister, noted merchant, mayor, and founder of San Jose's city library.

A horse-drawn trolley car pictured in front of the Hensley Building at the northwest intersection of Market and Santa Clara Streets, c. 1875. The Hensley Building housed a post office and a fire insurance company among other businesses on the ground floor. The sign on top of the trolley car advertises Spring's Auction House which was located at the northeast corner of Market and Santa Clara Streets.

Charles Doerr's New York Bakery, 437 First Street, in 1876 with delivery wagons in front. The Bakery, built c. 1863, was located on the east side of First Street between San Fernando and San Antonio on the present site of the Retail Pavilion.

This photograph of Crandell's Hotel on Market Street in the early 1870s shows the St. Joseph's Church structure that was built in 1869 in the background. The Crandell Hotel building later became the Pacific Hotel which was replicated at the San Jose Historical Museum in Kelley Park in 1977.

San Antonio Street, looking east from Second Street to the State Normal School building in 1876. The First Baptist Tabernacle is at the left with Temple Bikur Cholim, a Jewish synagogue, beyond. At the right of the photograph is the First Congregational Church. In the center is the original Normal School building, destroyed by fire on February 10, 1880.

Looking north from the Electric Light Tower in the early 1880s. Market Street is on the right with the Swiss Hotel facing it. San Pedro Street is on the left. The Fallon House, with many trees in the front yard, is at left center facing San Pedro. The First Ward School appears prominently in the upper left corner of the photograph.

Looking north on First Street between San Fernando and Santa Clara Streets. The I.O.O.F. building is at the right, housing A. A. Sage Groceries. O'Brien's Candy Factory can be seen at the center of the photograph which was taken about 1885. The street was paved in 1890.

San Jose's Chinatown on Market
Street prior to the fire which destroyed it in 1887. This Chinatown
was on the present site of the
Fairmont Hotel.

Looking south down Market Street
at the Plaza, c. 1882. This photograph was probably taken from St.
Joseph's Church. Chinatown is
located in the left center of the
photograph.

Santa Clara Street, looking west from Second Street, in the early 1880s. The new Electric Light Tower stands prominently at Market Street. A horse-drawn trolley car can be seen in the center of the photograph.

Dawn of A New Century
1886-1906

First and Santa Clara Streets were at the center of commercial activity during this period. Downtown San Jose featured numerous large banks (in the mid-1880s all four corners of First and Santa Clara were occupied by banks), distinctive churches and hotels, and a large new City Hall built in 1887 in the Plaza. Commercial buildings constructed at this time were often large city blocks of elaborate design and detail. Architects who left their mark on Downtown San Jose included the Lenzen brothers and Levi Goodrich.

By 1890 the population of San Jose was over 18,000. The Letitia Building (which still stands) was built in 1890 at 68 South First Street, the Hall of Records across from St. James Park in 1892, and a new Post Office building at Market and San Fernando in 1894. Five miles of pavement was laid in the business district of Downtown San Jose in the decade of the 1890s.

Automobiles arrived about the turn-of-the-century. Clarence Letcher opened what was said to be the first garage in the West in 1900 while George Osen and William F. Hunt made a half dozen "Osen & Hunt Specials" in their bicycle shop on Second Street the same year. In 1902 San Jose vied with San Francisco for the lead in auto ownership on the west coast with some 45 lucky owners.

Looking south on Market Street from St. John, c. 1905. On the left is the J. S. Williams clothing store next to the Palm Restaurant and the New York Exchange Hotel. City Hall (built in 1887) is in the center of the Plaza in the background. The Electric Light Tower, 237 ft. high, spanned Market and Santa Clara Streets from 1881-1915.

President McKinley visited San Jose on May 13, 1901 and spoke to a large crowd gathered in St. James Park. When he was assassinated four months later, the community erected a statue of the slain President, created by Rupert Schmidt, in memory of his visit.

President Theodore Roosevelt also traveled to San Jose during this period. He spent the night here in his private car and addressed a large gathering at the railroad depot at North Market and Bassett Streets on May 12, 1903.

On the morning of April 18, 1906 a devastating earthquake struck the Bay Area and caused considerable damage to Downtown San Jose. Buildings destroyed during the earthquake included the three-story Phelan building at First and Post, stores along Santa Clara and Lightston, and the new St. Patrick's Church. The top of the steeple fell off the Post Office building (now the Museum of Art) and heavy damage was sustained by the State Normal School, the First Presbyterian Church, and the new Hall of Justice. The accompanying fires were quickly extinguished, however, and the City soon returned to normal and began to rebuild. Within two years all signs of the earthquake's destructive force had disappeared.

St. Joseph's Church, shortly after it was completed according to architect Bryan Clinch's plans, in 1885. This is the third parish Church of St. Joseph located on the northeast corner of Market and San Fernando Streets. Designed in the shape of an equal-armed Greek cross, the church features twin bell towers and a lofty dome.

Construction began in 1887 on San Jose's new City Hall in the Plaza. Designed by the architect Theodore Lenzen, it housed the jail on the ground floor, council chambers on the main floor, and a public library on the third floor. This City Hall continued in use until it was demolished in 1958.

Trinity Episcopal Church on North Second and St. John Streets was built in 1863 and underwent a major remodeling in 1896. This photograph was taken by Andrew P. Hill after 1884 when the tower with the steeple and spire were added. The steeple pictured to the left of Trinity's was that of the First Presbyterian Church.

The First Unitarian Church on North Second Street across from St. James Park was built in 1891-92. Photographed by A. P. Hill, this building, designed by G. W. Page in Romanesque Revival style, is the only 19th Century structure fronting on St. James Park today whose facade is essentially unchanged.

Looking southeast from the Electric Light Tower in the 1880s. The second San Jose Normal School building stands prominently in Washington Square. The distinctive buildings at the center of the photograph are facing First Street, south of Santa Clara Street.

San Jose in late 1887 or 1888, looking northeast across a burned out Chinatown, present site of the San Jose Museum of Art and the Fairmont Hotel. A corner of St. Joseph's Church can be seen at the far left of the picture. Spires of the First Presbyterian Church are visible in the center of the photograph.

Looking south on Market Street from City Hall in the Plaza, 1890. In the center of the picture is the Eagle Brewery at Market and San Carlos Streets, the present site of the St. Claire Hotel. To the right is the Swedish Lutheran Emmanuel Church situated at the northwest corner of Market and Auzerais.

This photograph of a parade passing the intersection of Second and Santa Clara Streets was taken in 1890. The Porter Building on the east side of Santa Clara Street is under construction, next to the building housing the Women's Relief Corps, an auxiliary of the Grand Army of the Republic. The Horizon Center is located today on the site of the Porter Building.

The Letitia Building as it appeared at 68 South First Street in the 1890s. There were furnished rooms upstairs and businesses on the ground floor. Note the men working on the track below. The Letitia Building is one of the few grand old buildings still standing among the new structures in downtown San Jose.

Photograph taken in 1898 of the San Jose Post Office, built four years earlier. Located on Market Street at San Fernando, the building serves today as the San Jose Museum of Art. The peak on the clock tower was destroyed in the 1906 earthquake.

A granite monument with a bronze statue of William McKinley was unveiled on February 21, 1903, to mark the spot where the President stood to address a crowd on the west side of St. James Park on May 13, 1901. The statue still stands prominently in the Park. The St. James Hotel, which can be seen through the trees, is where the Post Office is today.

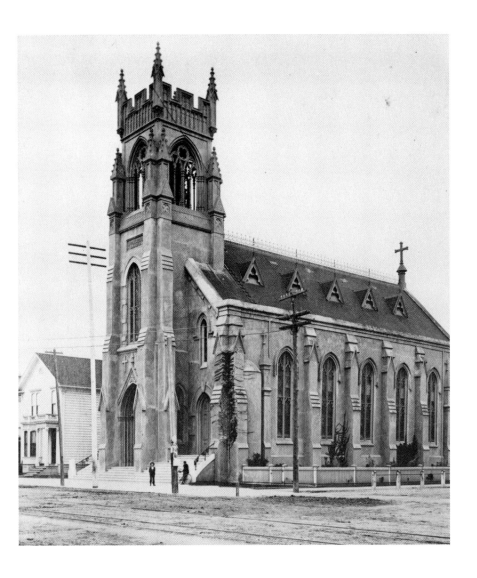

St. Patrick's Church on the northwest corner of East Santa Clara and 9th Streets was built in 1879. Photograph was taken by Andrew P. Hill in the 1890s. Note the unpaved street and streetcar track along Santa Clara Street.

St. Patrick's after the Earthquake of 1906.

Phelan Building at 53 South First Street. Hobson's Clothing Store, in foreground, was completely destroyed in 1906 quake.

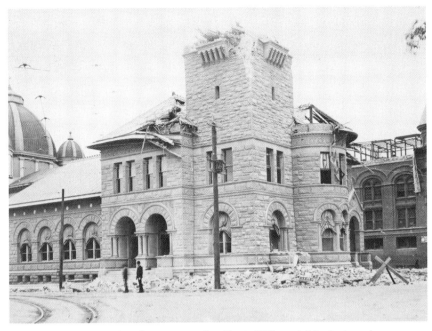

Earthquake damage to the Post Office at Market and
San Fernando Streets, 1906.

Earthquake damage to the Home Union building, 1906.

Earthquake damage to the Unique Theatre, 1906.

1906 Earthquake damage to San Jose High School built
in Washington Square in 1897-8.

Emergence of A Modern City
1907 - 1930

The period immediately following the earthquake was one of rapid growth and expansion as San Jose moved into the 20th Century. Residential areas sprang up in Naglee Park, the Hanchett District, and College Park while outlying areas such as the Gardner District and East San Jose were annexed to the City. A street improvement plan embarked upon in 1908 resulted in miles of new sidewalks, and numerous streetlights and intersection lights, mostly in the Downtown area.

On the cold, rainy morning of December 3, 1915, the famed Electric Light Tower, previously weakened in a series of storms, crashed into Santa Clara Street. Miraculously, no one was injured or killed in the collapse. The citizenry quickly determined that it was not economically feasible to rebuild the tower and, sadly, San Jose lost its well-known symbol.

During this time one man, more than any other, shaped the face of Downtown San Jose. Real estate developer T. S. Montgomery had the foresight to develop the City further to the south, along First Street from Santa Clara Street. Montgomery built the City's first "skyscraper", the Garden City Bank building at First and San Fernando Streets, as well as the Twohy Building, the Montgomery Hotel, the St. Claire Building, and the St. Claire Hotel. He also donated the land for the Civic Auditorium, built in 1934-36.

First Street, just north of Santa Clara Street, looking south, c. 1910. Bercovich's Cigar Store is on the northwest corner of the intersection in the Knox Block and the Garden City Bank and Trust is at the far left on the corner of First and San Fernando. The First National Bank building stands prominently at the southwest corner of First and Santa Clara. Note the variety of street transportation—horse and buggy, automobile, and trolley.

World War I saw San Joseans participating in a series of Liberty Loan Drives, parades, and other activities designed to promote and support the war effort. A Home Guard was formed and men from this city and county served in numerous companies.

The War proved to be a boon to Santa Clara County's fruit growing and packing industry, which mobilized to supply food for the troops in Europe in tremendous quantity. In addition to being known as the "prune capital of the world", by 1925 the Valley's reputation for other types of agriculture had reached a peak as well.

After the War the population of San Jose grew tremendously, from 39,642 in 1920 to 57,651 in 1930 — a 45% rate. Downtown development continued, with many of the City's most distinctive buildings dating from this period. The Bank of Italy (which changed its name to the Bank of America in 1930) built a $1,000,000 building in 1925-26 at the corner of First and Santa Clara Streets; the Trinkler-Dohrmann Building was constructed on First Street in 1926; and the 10-story Medico-Dental Building, designed by W. H. Weeks, was built in 1928.

By 1928 San Jose had 119 miles of paved streets and the distinction of having the greatest weekday automobile count of any city in the State. There was one car for every 2.92 people in Santa Clara County.

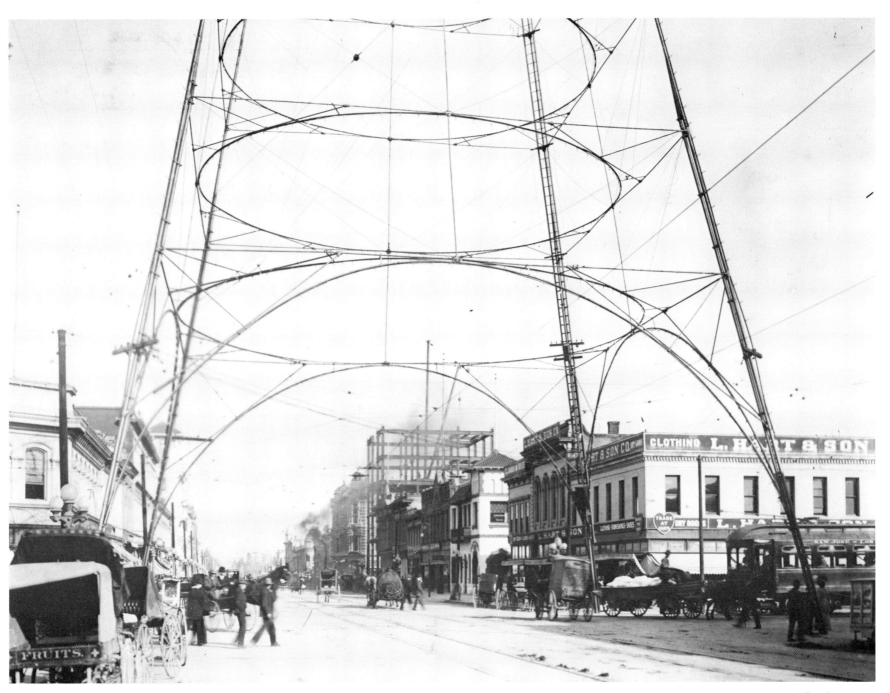

Looking east on Santa Clara Street under the Electric Light Tower at Market Street. Photograph, taken in 1909, shows the First National Bank building under construction on the southwest corner of First Street at Santa Clara. Note the Interurban streetcar northbound on Market Street at right of photo. The Electric Light Tower stood until December 3, 1915.

The First National Bank building at the southwest corner of First and Santa Clara Streets was refaced in 1961-63 and serves today as the Bank of the West.

An interested crowd gathers to watch the early stages of construction of the First National Bank building, 1909.

Bridge on Auzerais Street west of Vine collapsed during the big floods of March 1911. The original photo is dated March 7, 1911, and was taken looking east on Auzerais Street.

Clarence Letcher opened what was advertised as the first garage in California in 1900. This building, built in 1906 and shown here as it appeared in 1914 at 214 North First Street at St. James Street, was subsequently used by a variety of automotive-related businesses. In 1987 the building was remodeled for use as a nightclub, The Oasis.

The YMCA on the southeast corner of Santa Clara and Third Street. $160,000 was raised to build this structure which opened in May 1913, and still stands today.

In 1908 the Lyric Theater featured 5¢ moving pictures at 61 South Second Street. Portions of the theater front came from Grauman's Unique Theatre around the corner on East Santa Clara Street. Louis Lieber's Sign Shop was located upstairs.

The Garden City Bank building located on the corner of San Fernando Street at First Street, c. 1913. Building to the right is the Wilcox Building which was the original home of the Garden City Bank in 1887.

Onlookers enjoying a parade on July 4, 1914, as it passed in front of the Courthouse and the Hall of Records on First Street across from St. James Park.

The Sainte Claire Hotel, at Market and San Carlos Streets, opened October 16, 1926. It is shown here under construction.

The YWCA building, designed by Julia Morgan, was built in 1916 at the southeast corner of Second and San Antonio Streets. It contained a gymnasium, swimming pool, meeting rooms, cafeteria, and a small theater named Schofield Hall. In 1975 the building was demolished to make way for the San Antonio Plaza project.

The Montgomery Hotel was built by T. S. Montgomery on the southwest corner of San Antonio and South First Street in 1911. Today the Fairmont Hotel stands next to the Montgomery Hotel and the Retail Pavilion faces it.

First and Santa Clara Streets, looking north. The Beans Building on the right was home of the Bank of San Jose and was built after the old structure was damaged beyond repair in the 1906 earthquake. It was acquired by the Bank of Italy in 1927.

Armistice Day Parade in Downtown San Jose in 1919. O'Connor Sanitarium nurses paraded in their white uniforms.

First Street looking north, c. 1927. Addition to the First National Bank is under construction.

This photograph shows the early stages of construction on the Bank of Italy building at the southeast corner of First and Santa Clara Streets, 1927. The top of the City Hall and the dome of St. Joseph's Church can be seen in the background. The Bank of Italy's temporary branch is on the west side of First Street.

Looking south on First Street at the Bank of Italy under construction, 1927. To the left is the Knights of Columbus building, adjacent to the Commercial Building. The Beans Building is situated on the northeast corner of the intersection of First and Santa Clara.

The *Mercury-Herald* was a separately owned and operated daily morning newspaper from 1903 until 1942 when it merged with the *News*. The *News* was the afternoon paper and each had a separate staff. The *Mercury-Herald* building located at 30 West Santa Clara Street was acquired by the First National Bank in 1941. In the 1963 remodel, this building was incorporated into the First National Bank addition.

San Jose's Medico-Dental building was built on Santa Clara Steeet in 1928. It was designed by architect W. H. Weeks to house professional medical offices. The building is presently being remodeled into condominiums. W. H. Weeks also designed the De Anza Hotel, Herbert Hoover Junior High School and the Hotel Vendome, among other San Jose homes and commercial buildings.

Christmas shopping at Hart's on the southeast corner of Market and Santa Clara Streets in 1924.

First Street, on opening day of the new California Theater in 1927. The California Theater changed its name to the Fox Theater in 1955 and operated until c. 1970. Today the building awaits restoration.

Capital of the Valley of Heart's Delight
1931-1950

By 1930 "skyscrapers" and automobiles were commonplace in Downtown San Jose and all but a few of the outlying streets were paved. Many buildings of the previous century remained and blended with the new ones to house theaters, department stores, banks and businesses.

Downtown San Jose continued to be the commercial and economic hub of the county, which was known worldwide as "The Valley of Heart's Delight" for the enormous quantity of fruits and vegetables grown and processed here. In this agricultural-based community, the citizens were attracted to the Downtown for social and cultural activities as well as services.

On May 18, 1931 a disastrous fire gutted the stately old County Courthouse building on First Street, toppling the dome. When the building was remodeled the next year, a third story was added, the classical facade was altered, and the dome was not replaced.

The St. James Hotel, located next to the Courthouse at First and St. John, was torn down to make way for a new Post Office building. Shortly thereafter, the old Post Office on Market Street became the new home of the San Jose Public Library.

An aerial photograph of Market Street and Plaza Park, c. 1936. The Civic Auditorium was new. City Hall dominates the center of the Park.

On November 9, 1933 the citizens of San Jose were shocked by the kidnapping and brutal murder of Brooke Hart, son of the Hart's Department Store family. The subsequent lynching of the two murder suspects by an angry mob in St. James Park on November 26th brought notoriety and national attention to San Jose. No arrests were made in the lynching. The two trees in St. James Park, from which the suspects were hung, were quickly chopped down, but the whole affair had a lasting effect on the community.

During the decade of the 1930s San Jose suffered, like other cities across the country, from the Great Depression. One of the casualties of the era was the system of streetcars that had served the City. On April 10, 1938 the system was abandoned in a farewell celebration that featured free rides for all citizens from 9:00 PM to midnight. Seventy years of rail service through the City, dating back to horsecars and early electric cars, came to an end that night.

The population of San Jose in 1930 was approximately 60,000 people. By 1940 that number had jumped to almost 70,000.

After the attack on Pearl Harbor and America's entry into World War II, the influx of military personnel into the area was dramatic. Over one-half million people were brought into northern California during the course of the War, and two-thirds of them stayed on when their duty was completed. This massive surge of population would have profound effects on the San Jose area in the years to come.

Looking north on Market Street from City Hall in Plaza Park, c. 1930. The statue of Henry Cogswell (lower left) stood in the Park from 1887 until 1934. Cogswell was a San Francisco dentist and prohibitionist who donated drinking fountains topped with statues of himself to numerous cities.

Fiesta de las Rosas Parade, 1932. Elaborate flower-bedecked float moves down South First Street past the Hotel Curtis. The Fiesta de las Rosas was held for six years from 1926 to 1932.

On December 11, 1932, more than an inch of snow fell in San Jose.

Lynching of one of the two young kidnappers of Brooke Hart in St. James Park on November 26, 1933. A frenzied mob broke into the nearby jail, seized the pair, and dragged them to the Park where they were hanged.

The United States Post Office, designed by architect Ralph Wyckoff, at First and St. John Streets was built in 1933 at a cost of $308,000. It was built on the site of the old St. James Hotel. This structure across from St. James Park, continues to function as a United States Post Office to this day.

The County Courthouse after it was remodeled following the fire in 1931. A third story was added, the dome was not replaced, and the columns were recessed into the facade.

Construction of the San Jose Civic Auditorium took place during 1934-36. The structure cost $500,000 and was opened to the public on July 14, 1936.

The Civic Auditorium as it appeared new in 1936. The Montgomery Theater was named for T. S. Montgomery, who donated the land and a portion of the funding for the Civic Auditorium.

The Hotel Sainte Claire in its heyday, c. 1937. Built at a cost of $900,000, the six-story hotel was the city's finest when it opened October 16, 1926.

First Street, looking south, in the 1930s. The Beans Building is on the northeast corner of Santa Clara Street where Roos Brothers later stood. Bank of America building dominates the scene. Further south can be seen Blum's, a woman's apparel store, and Herold's Shoe Store.

Looking west down a bustling Santa Clara Street in the late 1940s. The DeAnza Hotel can be seen in the background. Designed by W. H. Weeks, the Hotel was built in 1931. Roos Brothers was now on the corner of First and Santa Clara with Penney's across the street.

Students from San Jose State's Eckert Hall parade through the Downtown business district on their way to the telegraph office and the Registration Board for "R-Day" at the beginning of World War II. A Bill Regan photograph from the collection of Leonard McKay.

The USO House in Plaza Park served many servicemen and women on leave during World War II and in the years that followed. A Bill Regan photograph from the collection of Leonard McKay.

Washington Square, San Jose State College, c. 1944. This was the site of the State Normal School founded in 1870. The Tower and "Quad" were built about 1909-10. Today only Tower Hall remains of the historic structures.

Looking north on First Street, late 1940s. Note two theaters, the State and the Mission, among the variety of businesses and services available.

Photograph taken in 1944 from the Bank of America building at First and Santa Clara Streets. Looking east toward the snowcapped hills, the Medico-Dental building dominates the scene. Center foreground on the south side of Santa Clara is the YMCA building.

Looking north on Second Street in 1946. "Jesus Saves" sign at right was on top of the First Baptist Church at Second and San Antonio Streets. Second Street had not yet been cut through St. James Park (the trees at the top center of the photograph).

A City in Transition
1951 - 1981

In the 1950s San Jose was the "Valley of Heart's Delight", the fruit producing and processing capital of the world. By 1980 the inexorable forces of population growth and the electronics industry had changed the character of the City. The Santa Clara Valley had gained new fame as "Silicon Valley".

The years immediately after World War II found local political leaders and businessmen launching an energetic campaign to attract new industry to San Jose and pushing for the expansion of freeways. San Jose was located in a prime geographic position as thousands of people, exposed to northern California during the War, chose to relocate here. The pro-growth and aggressive annexation policies of San Jose city government, coupled with new jobs in electronics, resulted in a tremendous surge of population. In 1950 San Jose had 95,280 residents living in 17 square miles. By 1960 the population of the city was 204,196 in a total of 64 square miles.

Outside the core area, extensive new home building occured to support the growth in population. Suburban shopping centers that emphasized convenience and ease of parking began to spell the downfall of the Downtown. In 1955, Sears & Roebuck departed for its new location on San Carlos Street and in 1958 Valley Fair Shopping Center opened. Another blow was struck when the City Hall moved to its present site at North First and Mission Streets in 1958.

Looking north on First Street from San Fernando Street, c. 1955. Note the busy sidewalks and the pedestrians crossing the intersection on the diagonal.

As early as 1956 business leaders were pushing for urban renewal to combat the classic decay that was beginning to be evident in the central area. An Urban Renewal Agency was subsequently formed to receive federal funds and plan for new development.

By the early 1960s the historical role of the Downtown as the center of trade and commerce in the Santa Clara Valley had declined substantially. In this regard San Jose was not unlike urban centers throughout the country which were finding that their traditional roles had changed.

In "Goals for San Jose" developed by City staff and citizen groups and adopted by the City Council in September 1961, it was the community's expressed desire to "Create and maintain an attractive central core, and make it the cultural, financial, commercial and entertainment center of the South Bay." But by 1970 every department store in Downtown San Jose had closed or moved elsewhere and San Jose was a study in urban sprawl. Much of the land that had been cleared for urban renewal remained vacant.

Gradually improvement began. By 1970 the first project of the Redevelopment Agency, Park Center Plaza, was being developed as a major financial center for San Jose and the formation of the San Antonio Plaza project had begun. The Center for the Performing Arts was completed in December 1971 and a seven-story library building on San Carlos Street was opened in 1970. The former post office/library building on Market Street became the new home of the San Jose Museum of Art, and in 1972 a million dollar renovation of the venerable old County Courthouse building occurred. A Convention Center was built as an addition to the Civic Auditorium in 1978.

By 1975 San Jose could boast that it was the regional headquarters for five of the nation's twenty largest banks. Between 1970 and 75 eight major highrise buildings were constructed Downtown, although efforts to attract a major hotel, residential complexes and retail shopping had failed.

By 1979 San Jose had grown to be the 17th largest city in the nation and the population by 1980 reached 625,763.

The south side of San Antonio Street, between First and Market Street, in 1957. These businesses, including Blossom Floral Shop, Cope & McPhetres Sport Shop and Sunsweet, had to vacate the premises for urban renewal by 1973. Photo courtesy of Blossom Floral Shop.

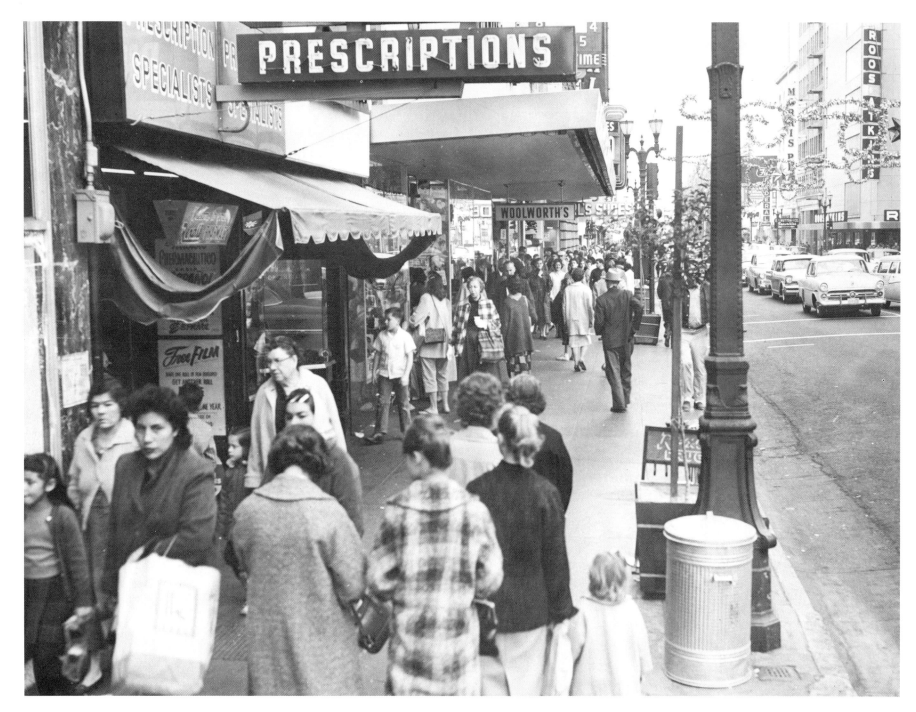

Looking north to Santa Clara Street on First Street, December 1959. Photograph clearly illustrates that Downtown San Jose was the shopping center of the region.

The south side of San Fernando Street, between First and Market Streets, c. 1959. A wide variety of businesses and services were available for Downtown shoppers.

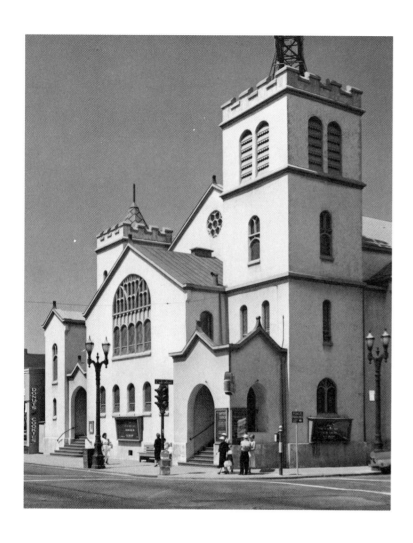

The First Baptist Church at the northeast corner of Second and San Antonio Streets, c. 1955. Founded in 1850, the church was located on this corner from 1859 to 1970. This particular building dated from 1908 and was razed to make way for the San Antonio Mall. A sign proclaiming "Jesus Saves" was a landmark on the roof of the church for years. Radio station KQW, which later became KCBS, was born here as a medium for spreading the word of God.

David Jack's Jose Theater was built on South Second Street in 1904. Shown here c. 1955, the Jose Theater still stands, awaiting restoration.

Santa Clara Street at the intersection of Market, c. 1959. Hart's department store was a landmark on the southeast corner. The Tower Saloon across the street is the only reminder of the Electric Light Tower that straddled the intersection from 1881-1915.

This January 1963 photograph shows the First National Bank at the southwest corner of First and Santa Clara Streets undergoing "modernization."

The Bank as it appeared upon completion of the renovation. The three-story section to the right was originally the *Mercury Herald* building. The First National Bank became the Bank of the West in 1979.

Downtown San Jose, looking north at Plaza Park, c. 1965. The City Hall was demolished in 1958 and traffic can be seen travelling on San Antonio Street through the Park. The new civic center complex north of Downtown is at the top of the photograph.

Downtown San Jose, looking southeast from approximately Santa Clara and Delmas Streets, c. 1968. Entire blocks were leveled in preparation for the Park Center Plaza redevelopment project. The Guadalupe River winds its way through the area to the right of the photograph. Photo by Del Carlo Photography.

The Center for the Performing Arts designed by Taliesin Associates, the successors to Frank Lloyd Wright, under construction, c. 1971. The Wells Fargo Bank, Bank of America, and the Union Bank have been completed in Park Center Plaza. The first of the Horizon Center towers can be seen behind the old Bank of America building. Photo by Del Carlo Photography.

The San Jose Main Library shortly after it opened in 1970. The building was designed to house 500,000 books and includes facilities for special collections.

The Pacific Telephone building addition under construction, c. 1972. More of the buildings in the Park Center Plaza project have been completed, but the lots along Almaden Boulevard are still vacant. Photo by Del Carlo Photography.

The skyline of Downtown San Jose beyond the newly-constructed freeway interchange, c. 1975. The Center for the Performing Arts, the Telephone building, and the Horizon Center have been completed. Photo by Del Carlo Photography.

May 1981 view of the east side of Market Street across from Plaza Park. The early site of Chinatown and later commercial buildings, this became the location for the Fairmont Hotel in 1987. The row of stores that can be seen along First Street was replaced by the Retail Pavilion. Photo by Sharon Hall.

Looking northwest at Downtown from Fourth and San Carlos Streets in 1981. The State Buildiing is under construction between Second and Third Streets at the left of the photograph. San Jose State University's Men's Gym is on the right. Photo by Sharon Hall.

June 1981 view of the Montgomery Hotel facing First Street, with the Twohy Building (now called the El Paseo Building) to the right. The Federal Building now occupies the area in the left foreground of the photograph. Photo by Sharon Hall.

Looking west along San Fernando Street, between Second and Third Street in 1981. The basements of demolished commercial structures lie exposed on the south side of the street. Photo by Sharon Hall.

The San Antonio Plaza Fountain in April 1981. The photograph, by Sharon Hall, was taken looking west from the top of the fountain toward Second Street.

Looking east on Santa Clara Street from the old Bank of America building at First Street. The Horizon Center towers are on the left. The First Methodist Church and the Medico-Dental building can be seen further down the street. Photo by Sharon Hall.

An Urban Renaissance
San Jose Today

San Jose in 1988 is a city with an impressive new skyline to match its position as the fourteenth largest city in the United States. Rising out of the rubble of structures demolished a decade or more ago, Downtown San Jose today is again becoming the commercial and cultural center of the Santa Clara Valley.

In 1980 the City of San Jose began an ambitious new redevelopment program which sought to combine public funds with private investment to revitalize blighted areas. Much of the effort was focused on the Downtown. Today San Jose has earned the reputation of having one of the most effective redevelopment programs in the nation.

The thrust of activity for the past decade has been to create a Downtown that is vibrant and alive, and to integrate economic activities with the amenities that make a city a pleasant place to live and work. Rejuvenated parks, pedistrian arcades, trees, theaters, museums, and public artwork have been planned and are being created to enhance the environment.

Perhaps the most visible symbol of San Jose's downtown renaissance is the $120 million Fairmont Hotel on Market Street which opened in 1987. Other new and significant commercial buildings, such as the first of the River Park Towers, the Market Post Tower, the office structures at

A light rail vehicle travels north on Second Street, approaching St. James Park. The spires of the Bank of America Building and Trinity Episcopal Church rise in the background. Photograph by Eric Penn.

Sixty South Market Street, Ten Almaden, and the Silicon Valley Financial Center carve a distinctive profile on the skyline.

Combined with the new construction is the renovation of significant historic buildings which provide continuity and complement the modern architecture. St. Joseph's Church, the Knox-Goodrich 1889 Building, the New Century (Saratoga Capitol) Block, the Scottish Rite Temple (San Jose Athletic Club), and the Moir Building are all examples of important old structures that have been, or are currently, being restored for modern use.

The fourteen-block transit mall along First and Second Streets is the centerpiece of a twenty mile-long light rail system that will soon link the Downtown to outlying residential areas and bring people into town for work, shopping and cultural activities. Restored historic trolleys will circle the transit mall, providing a colorful reminder of San Jose's past.

Much more development is planned and many amenities are still to be added, but the dramatic physical changes that have occurred have already brought a change in spirit. Citizens of San Jose look with pride on their Downtown and identify with it as the attractive and exciting center of urban life in the Santa Clara Valley.

An aerial view of Downtown San Jose taken early in 1988 shows Plaza Park and the surrounding buildings. An area still to be developed is at the right of the photograph, but the Fairmont Hotel has been completed and the Silicon Valley Financial Center is under construction. Photograph by Duane R. Stevens.

Looking down on the restoration of St. Joseph's Church from the Fairmont Hotel. The Silicon Valley Financial Center tower is under construction at right. Photograph by Alan E. Tenes.

River Park Tower stands above the east bank of the Guadalupe River. Photograph by Eric Penn.

The Bank of America building is reflected in the glass of the modernized J. C. Penney building on the northeast corner of First and Santa Clara Streets. Peering over the top, and seeming to blend into the reflection of the Bank of America building, is the Commercial Building on North First Street. Photograph by David G. More.

The Fairmont Hotel and the Silicon Valley Financial Center Tower rise above the Retail Pavilion. Photograph, by Barbara J. Dorr, was taken from the San Antonio Plaza fountain.

San Pedro Square, opening onto Santa Clara Street, is an area of restored buildings housing restaurants, night clubs, bookstores, and galleries. The old Farmer's Union building, now occupied by the Sizzler restaurant, is on the left. Photograph by Jacqueline M. Schuette.

Post Street, between Market and First Streets. Prior to 1902, Post Street was known as El Dorado Street. Photograph by Barbara J. Dorr.

The Transit Mall along First Street accommodates light rail vehicles and automobiles, as well as historic trolleys, buses and pedestrians. The Retail Pavilion is on the left with the El Paseo Building behind it. Photograph by Chris Laraway.

The Federal Office building on Second Street, designed by Hellmuth, Obata and Kassabaum Inc., and built in 1984. Photograph by Barbara J. Dorr.

The New Century Block on the southeast corner of Second and Santa Clara Streets was built in 1880 by Adolf Pfister, a prominent San Jose businessman who served three times as the city's mayor. The building was renovated in 1985-86 and the name was changed at that time. Photograph by Jacqueline M. Schuette.

The portico from the Eagles Hall building on Third Street, facing St. James Park, was all that was preserved when a large office building was constructed on the site in 1985. Photograph by Wayne MacRostie.

Looking east on Santa Clara Street in 1988. The Hotel DeAnza, the art deco building on the left, was named after the Spanish explorer Juan Bautista DeAnza. It was built in 1931, fell into disrepair in the 1960s, and closed for repairs in 1981. The rounded facade of the Ten Almaden office building is on the right. Photograph by Don Bender.

The St. Claire Club building, on the northeast corner of St. James and Second Streets, was designed by A. Page Brown. It was built in 1893 by Senator James Phelan as a private social club, a use which continues to this day. Photograph by Barbara J. Dorr.

Ten Almaden and the Commercial Center Bank building stand prominently at the intersection of Santa Clara Street and Almaden Boulevard. The Pacific Valley Bank building and parking structure can be seen in the reflection. Photograph by Everett Groux.

Market Street, just north of Plaza Park, with the Museum of Art building on the right and the Market Post Tower in the background. Photograph by Wayne MacRostie.

The Center for the Performing Arts is situated on Park Avenue at Almaden Boulevard. The River Park Tower and Clock Tower structures rise behind it. Photograph by Barbara J. Dorr.

Original Joe's, a San Jose tradition, is located in the St. Claire Building at First and San Carlos Streets. Photograph by Len Bruffett.

Shopping area in South Second Street is typical of the Vietnamese businesses that have flourished in Downtown San Jose since the mid-1970s. Photograph by Robert Shields.

Looking north on First Street from Post Street at the blend of old and new structures and the Transit Mall. The ornate building at lower right is the Knox-Goodrich building which was built in 1889. Photograph by Barbara J. Dorr.

A light rail vehicle travelling south on the First Street Transit Mall past the Ryland Block. Photograph by Than Trong Sy.

Looking across a vista of urban landscape and highrise bank and office towers in the financial center. Photograph was taken from Almaden Boulevard, looking east. Photograph by Chris Laraway.

Looking southwest, the DeAnza Hotel is reflected in the Commercial Center Bank building on Santa Clara Street. The stainless steel tube scupture on the median of Almaden Boulevard was designed by Stephanie Scuris. Photograph by Barbara J. Dorr.

Aerial view of the Convention Center under construction clearly shows its size in relation to surrounding buildings. The Center will contain thirty-one theater-style rooms and 425,000 square feet of exhibit space. The Holiday Inn, Civic Auditorium and San Jose Public Library are at the top of the photo facing San Carlos Street. Photograph by Duane R. Stevens.

Aerial view of Downtown looking southeast. The new Convention Center is under construction in right center. Photograph by Duane R. Stevens.

The Peralta Adobe, the earliest structure remaining in Downtown San Jose, is framed by a gate bearing the Peralta family's brand. The Adobe, located on St. John Street, dates from before 1800. Photograph by Barbara J. Dorr.